CONTENTS

CHOICE
Paul Muldoon • *Joy in Service on Rue Tagore* • Faber

RECOMMENDATIONS
Hannah Copley • *Lapwing* • Pavilion Poetry
Harry Josephine Giles • *Them!* • Picador
Jackie Kay • *May Day* • Picador
Tamar Yoseloff • *Belief Systems* • Nine Arches Press

SPECIAL COMMENDATION
Imtiaz Dharker • *Shadow Reader* • Bloodaxe Books

TRANSLATION CHOICE
Karin Karakaşlı • *Real* • Poetry Translation Centre
Translated by Canan Marasligil with Sarah Howe

PAMPHLET CHOICE
Jay Bernard, Will Harris, Mary Jean Chan, Nisha Ramayya • *Siblings* • Monitor Books

Poetry Book Society

CHOICE SELECTORS RECOMMENDATION SPECIAL COMMENDATION	JO CLEMENT & ROY McFARLANE
TRANSLATION SELECTOR	SHIVANEE RAMLOCHAN
PAMPHLET SELECTORS	NINA MINGYA POWLES & ARJI MANUELPILLAI
CONTRIBUTORS	SOPHIE O'NEILL MEGAN ROBSON LEDBURY CRITICS REBECCA MORLEY
EDITORIAL & DESIGN	ALICE KATE MULLEN

Poetry Book Society Memberships

Choice
4 Books a Year: 4 Choice books & 4 *Bulletins* (UK £65, Europe £85, ROW £120)
World
8 Books: 4 Choices, 4 Translation books & 4 *Bulletins* (£98, £160, £190)
Complete
24 Books: 4 Choices, 16 Recommendations, 4 Translations & 4 *Bulletins* (£230, £290, £360)

Single copies of the *Bulletin* £12.99

Cover Artwork Anna Mckeever @anna_mckeever annamckeever.com
Copyright Poetry Book Society and contributors. All rights reserved.
ISBN 9781913129668 ISSN 0551-1690

Supported using public funding by
ARTS COUNCIL ENGLAND

FSC MIX Paper from responsible sources FSC® C014866

Poetry Book Society | Milburn House | Dean Street | Newcastle upon Tyne | NE1 1LF
0191 230 8100 | enquiries@poetrybooksociety.co.uk

WWW.POETRYBOOKS.CO.UK

LETTER FROM THE PBS

I am writing just off the back of the Newcastle Poetry Festival – what an event! The sun peeped out from behind the endless winter clouds and it was wonderful to meet so many Poetry Book Society members and such talented poets. And of course to sell some poetry books, so huge thanks to everyone who attended the festival, tuned in online or visited our festival bookshop. An enormous thank you to Alice and Meg who organised the International Poetry Symposium and bookshop with their usual aplomb.

The PBS has continued its international outreach in the last couple of months. In April, Alice and guest poet Fiona Benson represented the UK at The Lilac Poetry Salon, a ceremony celebrating the centenary of the meeting of the poets Tagore and Xu Zhimo in Beijing. I'm sure you will have seen this in our Friday newsletter, and it can be found on our website for those interested in this international poetry celebration. So strangely apt given the Tagore inspired title of our Choice this season from Paul Muldoon.

This Chinese journey follows PBS visits to India and partnerships with Kolkata Poetry Festival and Bhutan Book Festival over the last two years. What interests me in the work we do is the positive ripple effect from events, reviews, networking – most of which we will never fully know. Several of the poets who took part in Newcastle Poetry Festival were invited following connections made at Bhutan Book Festival. The PBS would never have been invited there if Alice hadn't taken part in a British Council fellowship between India and the UK – all testament to the truly international power of poetry!

Summer 2024 is a magnificent selection of poets and collections, and as ever, every book and poet has their own particular draw. I hope you enjoy the write-ups from both the selectors and the poets themselves as much as I have, and you are inspired to read the collections reviewed within. One last thing, Paul Muldoon will feature on our Summer Podcast in partnership with Arji's Poetry Pickle Jar – it's going to be brilliant, so please do give it a listen by scanning the QR code below.

SOPHIE O'NEILL
PBS & INPRESS DIRECTOR

PAUL MULDOON

Paul Muldoon was born in County Armagh in 1951. He now lives in New York. A former radio and television producer for the BBC in Belfast, he has taught at Princeton University for thirty-five years. He is the author of fifteen collections of poetry. Among his awards are the 1972 Eric Gregory Award, the 1980 Sir Geoffrey Faber Memorial Award, the 1994 T.S. Eliot Prize, the 1997 *Irish Times* Poetry Prize, the 2003 Pulitzer Prize, the 2003 Griffin International Prize for Poetry, the 2004 American Ireland Fund Literary Award, the 2004 Shakespeare Prize, the 2006 European Prize for Poetry, the 2015 Pigott Poetry Prize, the 2017 Queen's Gold Medal for Poetry, and the 2020 Michael Marks Award. He is a Fellow of the Royal Society for Literature and the American Academy of Arts and Letters.

JOY IN SERVICE ON RUE TAGORE

FABER | £14.99 (HB) | PBS PRICE £11.25

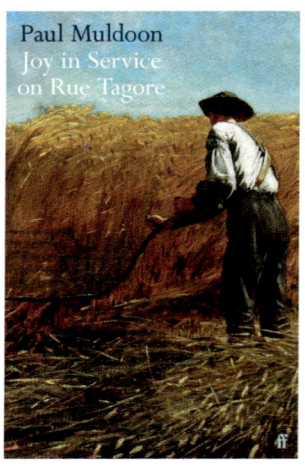

"He who fights with monsters should look to it that he himself does not become a monster. And when you gaze long into an abyss, the abyss also gazes into you."– Friedrich Nietzsche, *Beyond Good and Evil*

This quote opening Paul Muldoon's *Joy in Service on Rue Tagore*, prepares us for the monsters and acts of atrocity stalking humanity past and present. 'Near Izium' not only bears witness to the war in Ukraine but meticulously interweaves Putin with the massacre of Babi Yar (mass murder of the Jews of Kyiv in 1941) and the Greek myths of Bellerophon and Chimera. Muldoon uses rhyme, repetition and word-play with a griot's authority and acuity, to make known the horrors, ending with a curse:

> Let his pillow be stuffed with gorse
> and common broom.
> Let him find no rest in the bosom of Abraham
> but forever go off at half cock
> across the Dnieper in a six- or eight-oared black gig.
> Across the Dnieper. At half cock. A black gig.

There are poems with lyrical sequences, full of lament and questions like the villanelle 'The Belfast Pogrom: Some Observations'. Or 'When the Italians' another sequence of villanelles shining a light on the invasion of Libya, Mussolini and his execution. And yet there is joy to be found in this collection, 'Artichokes and Truffles' and 'Pablo Neruda: Ode to the Artichoke' playfully explore aspects of being human.

Muldoon's title poem 'Joy in Service on Rue Tagore' encapsulates the joy and relief of receiving good news, as part of a series of poems exploring the effects of cancer on both the writer and his mother from 'The MRI' to 'The Castle of Perseverance'. Muldoon's layered working of traditional forms bleeds and blends into each other, creating hybrids inviting us to look at poems in so many different ways, asking us how can we "gaze long into an abyss", knowing "the abyss also gazes into you"?

SELECTOR'S COMMENT

ROY McFARLANE

PAUL MULDOON

Like most of my poems, these ones snuck up on me. That includes even those pieces which might appear to be most premeditated, like the series of quaterns scattered through the book. This French verse form has an insidious, incessant refrain that is supremely well-suited to the insidious and incessant themes that seem to preoccupy my older self. There's 'By the Time You Read This', for example, which revisits the subject of 'Why Brownlee Left', the title poem of my 1980 collection. Or there's 'A Graveyard in New England', a musing on the odd phenomenon of clearing all but one field of stones.

The older self I mentioned is very much to the fore in another poem that avails of an inherited form, the sestina on 'The MRI', that mainstay of the medical test centre. Again, the sestina seems to be perfectly attuned to the obsessive rituals of aging and the comings and goings of human history from the Neanderthals to the neurosurgeons.

The title poem refers to the great Indian poet, Rabindranath Tagore, who once remarked that "I slept and dreamt that life was joy. I awoke and saw that life was service. I acted and behold, service was joy." I imagine the poem spoken by an old codger from a John Le Carre novel who has seen "service" in one or two unlikely spots. I might go so far as to say he's been involved in dirty tricks, possibly in the kind of state collusion we've seen all too often in my native Northern Ireland. I might go even further and mention that the detail of the hand kept in the fridge is drawn from an episode involving the Westies, an Irish gang once active in my adopted home town of New York.

PAUL RECOMMENDS

Ciaran Carson, *Collected Poems Volumes One and Two* (Gallery Books); Scott McKendry, *Gub* (Corsair Poetry); James Conor Patterson, *Bandit Country* (Picador); Medbh McGuckian, *The Thankless Paths to Freedom* (The Gallery Press); Stephen Sexton, *Cheryl's Destinies* (Penguin); Nick Laird, *Up Late* (Faber).

THE RIVER IS A WAVE

The river is a wave that never breaks
though it may briefly surge
as it edges its way out of that three-mile-long lake
in which it's managed to submerge

its ever so slightly diminished sense of hurt.
The river is a wave that never breaks
despite such fitful spurts
of "enthusiasm." Let's say, for argument's sake,

that if it follows in its own wake
to satisfy an imperfectly remembered urge,
the river is a wave that never breaks
but is forever on the verge

of confronting an issue it's inclined to skirt
since it's only the sea, with its incomparable ache,
that may categorically assert
the river is a wave that never breaks.

THE MOURNER

From deep within my grave
I must have been hoping to present less of a target
to those who would make me an object of grief.
The use of ergot

to loosen the birth knot
and generally bring on labor
had also proved invaluable to hastening my end.
That silent "b" in Lefebvre

bruited the space in which an archer might train
his ash arrow on an ash tree.
I was able to gauge this most recent arc

from the green stain
where a mourner had now gone down on one knee
the better to find his mark.

Image: Naomi Woddis

HANNAH COPLEY

Hannah Copley is a British writer, editor, and academic. She is a senior lecturer in Creative and Professional Writing at the University of Westminster and a poetry editor at *Stand* magazine. Hannah's first collection *Speculum* was published by Broken Sleep Books in 2021. Her poetry has appeared in *POETRY, Blackbox Manifold, The London Magazine, Poetry Birmingham, Stand, Under the Radar, Bath Magg*, and other publications and anthologies. Set against a backdrop of shifting fields and disappearing habitats, *Lapwing* explores personal and ecological grief and tells the story of a father and daughter forever at odds.

LAPWING

PAVILION PRESS | £10.99 | PBS PRICE £8.25

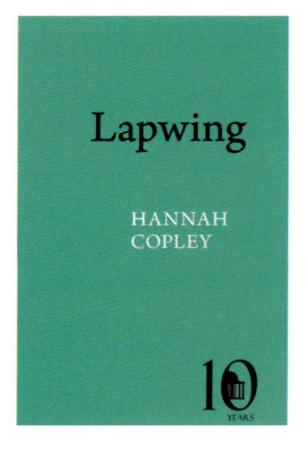

And she remembers his stories
    Lapwing, quenched,
slowly tumbling
from high singularity
into the scrape of his thoughts.

Voice and agency are given to the Lapwing, we enter into their world, their bodies, their minds and soul, speaking their language "panicked pees, weep weep / softening into prose." We are caught up in the conversations and thoughts of Peet and Lapwing, waxing lyrical about living and surviving in a world, overlapping birds and humans. We are carried away on a bird song.

'(I) Otherwise known as peewit' is part of an incantatory series of poems, interweaving its hymn like song through the collection, a myriad of known and lesser-known names and a declaration of self-awareness for this creature. A series of prose reports called 'Sighting' are a joy to read, collated over centuries in response to the Lapwing's appearance in unusual places or settings; "Newfoundland, November 1905; Canada, January 1927; Shemya, Alaska, 2006". In their world "Birds have their demons too." They live "amongst heron lording it on some nearby / log, the dull, incessant gossip of the coots: / chew-it, chew-it, chew-it." Lapwings dream, make phone calls, write letters, flick through videos, and visit a doctor.

The ever presence of danger is always felt, as in '(V) Come cat, he shrieks, come fox, come man', or 'Two Lines' with its constant awareness of "the tiny wind turbine", "a crucifix of propellor." Lapwings even have "family trees" from "One cousin exploded / while breaking on the Falkland Islands;" to "one ex-girlfriend roosting / somewhere in Kent." And there's a tenderness, love and loss that abounds through the collection as in 'Mnemonic technique', "I would imbue that blood trail if I could take it all back" and yet the heart is big enough to hold grief and enable us to stand tall in those moments.

        Here

        in the church of the heart
        lost objects abound. Here in the church
        of the heart
                I am the tallest thing for miles.

SELECTOR'S COMMENT | ROY McFARLANE

HANNAH COPLEY

Lapwing is a poetic biography of a bird and the word itself, but it is also a sideways and jagged attempt to understand addiction and the ways it can vanish a life. I see it as a book-length sequence made up of multiple, overlapping forms, but there are a few clear voices in conversation. The numerical poems are concerned with the titular figure of Lapwing, an enigmatic bird slowly disappearing beneath addiction and habitat loss. His journeying is interwoven with that of his daughter Peet and her attempts to locate and understand her vanished father. Circling their stories are recorded sightings of Lapwing by countless amateur ornithologists. Finally, there are the wordless lapwing flocks.

The voices of the book first took shape six years ago. There used to be a few lapwings that would arrive to nest in the fields near my house. I spent a lot of time walking with my newborn daughter strapped to my chest, listening to their strange cries, and watching them bounce around in song-flight as I tried to bounce her to sleep. As I walked, the voice of one particular lapwing set up shop in my head, and as I began to learn more about them, the poems took on a life and shape of their own.

Lapwings have a remarkable technique for evading predators. They will put on a show, they will tumble and swoop and cry out and hover. They may even dive at the attacker. They will do everything they can to distract and divert attention away from what makes them vulnerable. It is a masterful choreography of survival, and for centuries poets and playwrights misunderstood it as deceitful, cowardly behaviour. I imagine that many people who grew up with an alcoholic parent might recognise that dance around the truth. And perhaps the misunderstanding too.

>   Migration
> offers endurance, novelty, otherwise known as
> the hard-won maintenance of a myth, as survival.
> Dissemblance as another breed of song.

HANNAH RECOMMENDS

Everything by Fran Lock, Alice Notley, Bhanu Kapil, Anne Carson, and Deryn Rees-Jones; Zaffar Kunial, *England's Green* (Faber); Jason Allen-Paisant, *Self-Portrait as Othello* (Carcanet); Martha Sprackland, *Citadel* (Pavilion); Zeina Hashem Beck, *There Was and How Much There Was* (Smith|Doorstop); Jay Bernard, *Surge* (Chatto); Rebecca Tamás, *Witch* (Penned in the Margins); Anthony Joseph, *Sonnets for Albert* (Bloomsbury); Lawrence Illsley, *A Brief History of Trees* (Live Canon); Joe Carrick-Varty, *More Sky* (Carcanet); Carrie Etter, *Imagined Sons* (Seren); Tom Branfoot, *Boar* (Broken Sleep Books).

IN WHICH BEARS EAT HER

There she goes dreaming of a place un-held by gravity,
dreaming of a four-day week and the four-week course
in fashion management that she saw advertised on the side

of the moving machine, dreaming of bears that will eat you alive,
dreaming of moving around various stocks and shares
and consolidating all the pension pots into one manageable

and easily trackable account. The starlings are everywhere
and she's longing to sleep and not be so alive in her body,
to not be on the verge of busting out of her own feathers

in frustration. What is all this fuss, she thinks. From what
continent does anger migrate? Where does it summer?
Peet grinds her beak against the day's particular whetstone.

ON WAKING

Hawk hovers
and falls from the firmament.

Peet, roosting in dawn frost,
thinks of mornings

spent enveloped
in the cotton womb

of her grandparent's bed.
Grief, she thinks,

is just an inflammation
of memory;

a fine tendon
slowly ripping itself

from wingtip
to beak.

Image: Rich Dyson

HARRY JOSEPHINE GILES

Harry Josephine Giles is a writer and performer from Orkney. She holds an MA in Theatre Directing from East 15 Acting School and a PhD in Creative Writing from the University of Stirling. Her verse novel *Deep Wheel Orcadia* received the 2022 Arthur C. Clarke Award for Science Fiction Book of the Year. Her poetry collections – *Tonguit* and *The Games* – were shortlisted for the Edwin Morgan Poetry Award, the Forward Prize for Best First Collection, and the Saltire Poetry Book of the Year.

THEM!
PICADOR | £10.99 | PBS PRICE £8.25

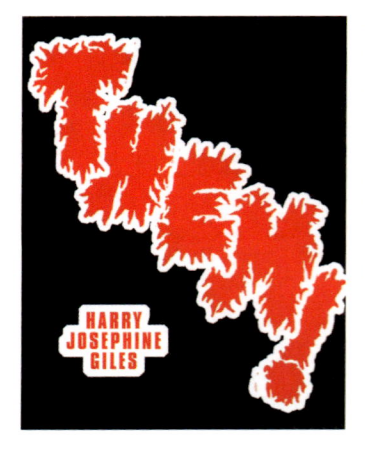

Like the Scottish primrose in its opening sequence, *Them!* flowers courageously on the cliff edge of a country failing its transgender citizens. At a time when promises to ban torturous conversion therapies are reneged, and trans existence is debated in so-called "gender wars", Harry Josephine Giles' skilful and seditious poems tune out from the hateful noise and into her rallying cry against injustice:

> the cry of an eagle
> or the cry of someone
> crying like an eagle
> or the cry of someone
> hoping for an eagle

The collection arrives synergistically with an American sister book. Judith Butler's *Who's Afraid of Gender?* describes the demonisation, shaming and neglect of trans people as "a patriarchal wet dream" and calls for "key texts" to be duly considered. *Them!* marks a new key text. Furious in its humanity and exceptional range of expression, the book documents how withheld healthcare can lead to dangerous self-medication ('The New Girl'). Elsewhere, the staggering and exquisite 'Elegy' grieves as punchlines are unapologetically spun from a child's murder. In the face of these deep sadnesses and frustrations, the poems retain the daring wit we discover in 'The Reasonable People':

> reasonable   The   have become   chapped
> people think   reasonable   so heated.   hands from
> it's important   people say it's The   so much
> to weigh the   such a shame   reasonable   washing. The
> arguments.   that things   people have   reasonable

Weaving between acronyms, explosive typography, directional reorientations and photography, the poetics of these formal experiments fearlessly bring to bear the complexities of transition. As in Monica Youn's strophic 'Study of Two Figures (Pasiphaë/Sado)', which dubs textual and fleshy forms "containers", the making of person and poem converges here. Giles' title poem draws further from Youn as its speaker tells us "the shape of a poem is the shape of a door", through which change can be engendered and safety secured. In the words of performance artist Travis Alabanza, "when I say trans, I mean escape". These exemplary poems are fire doors.

JO CLEMENT

HARRY JOSEPHINE GILES

The problem I'm faced with now, as that cursed and persistent thing, a trans woman in public, is how to write through the constraints of an overdetermined identity. This is not a new problem. As Amy Marvin writes in *The First Trans Poem*:

> Every
> decade is a new trans moment, the
> first trans literature... the first arrival
> of trans arrival.

What is happening now, though, is that the ancient newness of trans is being performed for an absurdly escalating chorus of bully journalists, bankrupt AGA activists, venal limpets on the drowned skerries of power, and triggered billionaires. Before I put fingers to keys, the meaning of my writing is already foreclosed. What remains, as Judith Butler said, all too unaware of what 4chan would make of the term, is to work the trap.

I wrote this book while injecting bootleg hormones into my thighs and listening to noise music. In Leah Tiger's essay on the centrality of trans women to noise music, *A Sex Closer to Noise*, she wrote that "In trans noise the experience of violence turns inward". There was nothing to do with the world's contempt but make it a scream that ripped my throat – but in that tearing is also my divine joy. My joy in my body, my sisterhood, my world. When I walk the hills in this praising body, swaddled in Gore-Tex, the wind off An Cuiltheann thudding like a lossy mp3, each painful step is a gift. One foot in front of the other. It's late February in Eilean a' Cheò, and the birds are beginning their spring songs, a cacophony of industrial drones sped up and pitch-shifted, and I know they're praising the beautiful, terrible things I've made of myself.

HARRY JOSEPHINE RECOMMENDS

Andrea Abi-Karam and Kay Gabriel (eds.), *We Want It All: An Anthology of Radical Trans Poetics* (Nightboat); Chase Berggrun, *R E D* (Birds, LLC); Jamie Berrout, *Essays Against Publishing*; Jos Charles, *Feeld* (Milkweed Editions); Callie Gardner, *Naturally It Is Not* (87 Press); Porpentine Charity Heartscape, *Eczema Angel Orifice*; Ava Hofman, *[...]*; Ava Hofman (ed.), *Sporazine 1 & 2*; Sybil Lamb, *I've Got a Time Bomb* (Topside Press); Never Angeline North, *Sea-Witch* (Inside the Castle); Nat Raha, *Of Sirens, Body & Faultline*s (Boiler House Press); Verity Sprott, *Prayers, Manifestos, Bravery* (Pilot Press); Laurel Uziell, *Instant Cop Death* (Shit Valley Press).

Image: Daisy Bates

I LOVE TO HEAR HER SPEAK

a cling peach slithering out from its tin

a lip gloss ground into paste by the teeth

a burnt clutch scribbling down from the pass

a cowpat drilled by extravagant heels

a hangnail snatching a lark by the throat

a wire thong under a cage crinoline

a crazed screen slicing a covetous thumb

a quotetweet high on the sodium moon

a plum duff smelting its thruppenny bit

a lightbulb loose in a bucket of knives

a string cheese stubbornly whole in the pipes

a war pig through the dimensional gate

a salt lick slapping a jellyfish sting

a blessed bass warily bowed at the bridge

Image: Denise Else

JACKIE KAY

Jackie Kay was born in Edinburgh. A poet, novelist and writer of short stories, she has enjoyed great acclaim for her work for both adults and children. Her novel *Trumpet* won the Guardian Fiction Prize. She has published three collections of stories with Picador, *Why Don't You Stop Talking*, *Wish I Was Here*, and *Reality, Reality*; two poetry collections, *Fiere* and *Bantam*; and her memoir, *Red Dust Road*. From 2016-21 she was the third modern Makar, National Poet for Scotland. She lives in Manchester and is Professor of Creative Writing at the University of Salford.

MAY DAY

PICADOR | £10.99 | PBS PRICE £8.25

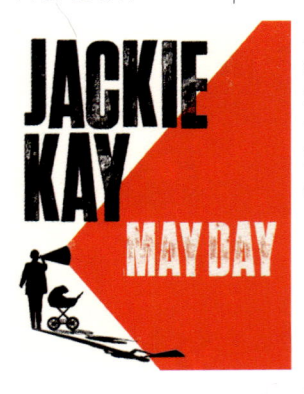

A collection full of song, love and protest, hidden stories, historical and personal, Jackie Kay's *May Day* is a vessel for holding grief but equally for pouring the emotional anguish, love lyrics are poured like libations across the page in memory of parents and ancestors.

> There's my father
> tartan blanket round his shoulder
> his staff in his right arm
>
> defending us,
> his black children on this island
> against all harm.

In 'Daughters, Neighbours' a shared grief is felt, "walking grief's long corridor / to the open window, the open door". In 'Blue Boat Mother', 'Three Little Birds' and 'My Mum is a Robin' Kay finds refuge in the world around her, nature takes the writer into her bosom and provides solace, as well as a gift to transcribe the moment and in transcribing we transcend death's painful grip.

Kay also transports us across time where we can hear and feel the power of Paul Robeson, Harry Bellefonte, Nina Simone and many more. She explores a life well lived in activism from Greenpeace, Iraq Wars to the present pandemic and Black Lives Matter. Kay's fine ear for voices and the vernacular of diverse people becomes a tool of activism as in 'A Banquet for the Boys':

> Tabbouleh since you're all trans-affirming bros.
> Halloumi to hail the halo round your afro.
> Zucchini since you're so queer-affirming,
> Makdous, moutabal for loving diversity and the mandem.

Kay often returns to her mother who can be found in the riverbed, in the birdsong, the empty table. There's a beautiful haunting in 'Still Life at Home', an assonance of grief in two parts.

> I've no known much but I huv known this:
> This sma' bit o' hoose I call ma hame.
> In the winter, the wind wails like a selkie
> who's had a wamefu o' the sea

And like a selkie the collection shapeshifts again to hold her father. *May Day* is a praise, a blues, a love letter to all those that have gone before.

ROY McFARLANE

JACKIE KAY

When I was a kid, I used to love going on the MAY DAY marches, from George Square in Glasgow to Queen's Park. I loved the camaraderie of it all, the sense of drama. The sudden appearance of the spectator, who left her perch behind the cordon to join in.

I was reminded of these marches when I saw Ingrid Pollard's wonderful exhibition at Glasgow Women's Library, *No Holds Barred*. As well as a huge photograph bustling with anti-racist protestors, Ingrid had interviewed the people whose photographs she'd taken. There were voice messages from many old friends. It took me back to all the demos I'd joined over my life and led to the long poem in *May Day,* 'A Life in Protest'.

> My brand-new mum carrying wee me.
> My brother in a pram pushed by Hugh MacDiarmid,
> black beret on, bead eyes, lined face,
> *but greet and in yer tears*
> *ye'll droon the hale clanjamfrie!*

I thought of my parents' long lives of protest; and how when they died, the one thing that comforted me was the beliefs they shared with many. I think of the people who come through the book, Nina Simone, Harry Belafonte, Paul Robeson, Fanny Eaton, as people joining them on a May Day Parade. For the person of no fixed religion, it was a solace to imagine that the dead still believe in peace after they have gone. I started thinking about what is left behind.

JACKIE RECOMMENDS

I've picked poets who have inspired this particular collection, who appear in direct or indirect ways in the pages of *May Day:* Douglas Dunn, *Elegies* (Faber); Audre Lorde, *The Black Unicorn* (Penguin); Roger Robinson, *A Portable Paradise* (Peepal Tree Press); Norman MacCaig, *The Collected Poems* (Chatto and Windus); Aimé Césaire, *Notebooks of a Return to My Native Land* (Bloodaxe); Victoria Adukwei Bulley, *Quiet* (Faber).

You are the voice from the future, suddenly, not the past: here to tell us something we struggle to hear.

Image: Neil Lang

LAST NIGHT I DREAMT OF PEGGY SEEGER

She was singing a peace song to my mum
even though she knew that my mum had gone
as if she believed the dead still believe
in peace after they have gone.
She was singing to the stars and the trees,
singing to the very air we breathe.
She was singing to the robins, blackbirds, bees,
to the grasses in the summer breeze,
singing to the hope we could all be agreed,
like all the peace songs that had gone before,
that this old world would put an end to war.

Last night I dreamt of Peggy Seeger.

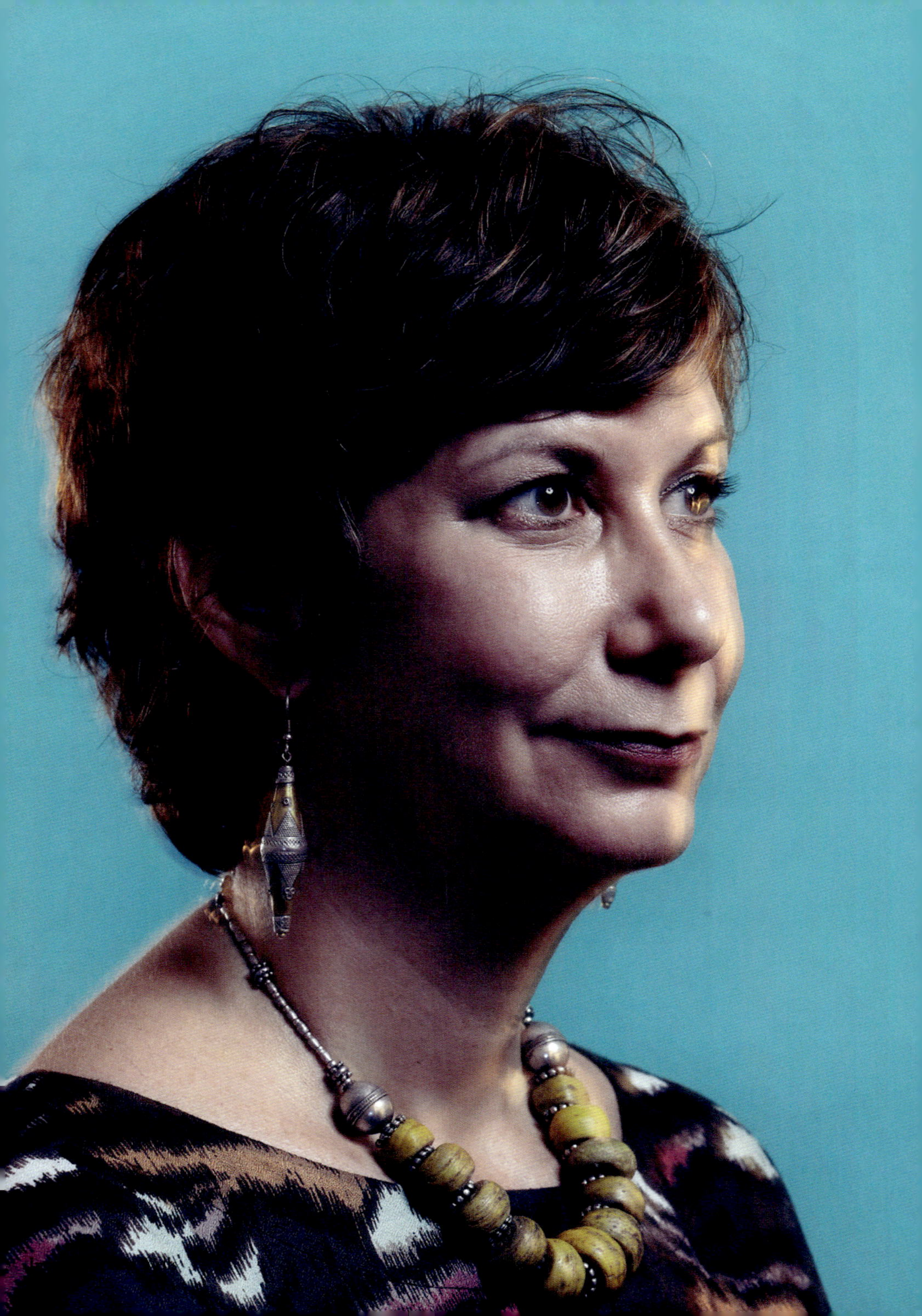

TAMAR YOSELOFF

Tamar Yoseloff has published six collections, including *The Formula for Night: New and Selected Poems* (2015) and most recently, *The Black Place* (2019), both from Seren. She's also the author of *Formerly*, a chapbook incorporating photographs by Vici MacDonald (Hercules Editions, 2012) shortlisted for the Ted Hughes Award; and collaborative editions with artists Linda Karshan and Charlotte Harker respectively. She was a lecturer on the Poetry School / Newcastle University MA in Writing Poetry and continues to teach independently. She received a Cholmondeley Award in 2023.

BELIEF SYSTEMS
NINE ARCHES PRESS | £12.99 | PBS PRICE £9.75

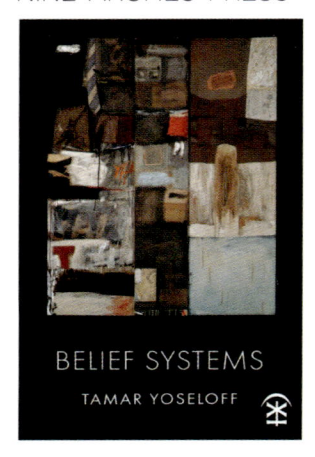

Belief Systems opens with an epigraph from John Cage's experimental lecture-in-performance, 'Where are we going? And what are we doing?' (1961). Cage's score synchronously plays four taped texts to suggest "meaninglessness as (the) ultimate meaning". The title poem interrogates this idea, as Yoseloff's lines are invisibly stitched with quotations from William Blake, Thomas Gray and John Latham. These unattributed lines correspond with Latham's "flat time" concept, in which all events are equal. Collage informs this collection, which invites readers to explore language liberated from its author, marvellously suggested by this line break in 'Canyon': "If the artist wasn't dead already he could be / arrested for causing harm". Each poem confidently leaps from visual artwork into Yoseloff's own imaginative territory. She describes her ekphrases fittingly as "hazy reflections rather than obedient mirrors". 'Combines' is a strong sequence illustrated by Robert Rauschenberg's mixed media artworks. The vocabulary of these artworks, including their titles, suggests each poem, such as 'Monogram':

> – schmuck, sucker, fall guy –
> he'll never be on top, never know
> what it's like to be truly prized. It's no
> ball being him. It really gets his goat.

The 'Field Companions' quartet responds to Alison Gill's 2021 sculptural installations with transcendental, trippy lyricism:

> ...you've abandoned
> your b**o**dy –
> it has no pur**p**ose anymore
>   its **p**onderous limbs and vexing organs
> gone

Sara Haq's prismatic drawing series on sensitive cognition 'Things I did that nobody noticed (but that changed everything)' provide the "pilot light" that sparks Yoseloff's dazzling 'Ignition'. Here, we're told a painful "name still / scalds (the speaker's) tongue" but the poem never fully lets the wound's nature slip. These memorable poems invite us to experience language voraciously on its terms. Like the speaker in 'Fault Lines' who reassembles a broken plate's "jagged bits", as readers interrogate this well-made, plucky collection, we "learn to live / with what is fractured".

SELECTOR'S COMMENT

JO CLEMENT

TAMAR YOSELOFF

My collection *Belief Systems* takes its title from a series of works by the British artist John Latham, who made sculptural assemblages from books covered in plaster and sprayed with black paint. Latham believed books contained both knowledge and error, and were therefore endlessly problematic. By presenting books as objects arrested in a static state, they become a present event for the viewer, while still containing the history of their subjects – an idea that Latham expanded in his theory of "flat time". The title poem was written in the month before we descended into the first lockdown, when I found myself immersed in the work of another artist, Robert Rauschenberg, who made constructions from found objects which he called 'Combines' (around the same time Latham was creating his book sculptures).

During those months of isolation, I found Rauschenberg's 'Combines' consoling; his gathering of human detritus – photographs, neckties, taxidermied birds, bits of furniture, etc. – became a scrapbook of his attempts to record existence. As I wrote about the 'Combines', other artists began to appear in the poems – Rauschenberg's collaborators John Cage and Merce Cunningham, his lover, Jasper Johns, as well as Joan Eardley, Eva Hesse, Mark Rothko and Christo – artists whose work and life are inexorably linked.

In writing about them, I was trying to locate the element that unites them – something to do with preservation, the idea that the things you make are intensely personal, but also have a life beyond you. Of course, poetry operates in the same way as Rauschenberg's and Latham's systems: the poem is a moment suspended in time, held up to the reader as an event which has already occurred, but continues to occur each time the poem is reread. I find that consoling too.

TAMAR RECOMMENDS

I am happy to be reading anything by Sean O'Brien, but when I want a quick fix of his brilliance, I turn to *Cousin Coat* (Picador) which contains a selection of his early work. Two books on legacy and inheritance are important to me: Annie Freud's beautiful *Hiddensee* (Picador) and Jacqueline Saphra's brave and bold *Velvel's Violin* (Nine Arches Press). *To Repel Ghosts* (Knopf) is an extraordinary book by the American poet Kevin Young which makes a profound connection with the work of Jean-Michel Basquiat.

Image: Robert Rauschenberg, *Summerstorm*, 1959. Michael and Judy Ovitz Collection, Los Angeles
©Robert Rauschenberg Foundation

SUMMER FIELDS

I very often find I'll take my paints to a certain place that has moved me and I'll begin to paint there and I find perhaps by the end of the summer I haven't moved from that place – my paintings are still there and I've worn a kind of mark in the ground - Joan Eardley

In the margin of land the farmer left unsown
cornflowers and daisies stake their ground,
alert heads raised to sun. This is the place
between wheat and wild where I will stand,
grass sticking to canvas, boots planted in dirt.
The sun is making gold of plain old hay,
and all I must do is make my mark, my hand
understanding what the mind can't grasp.

Glory be to field, to sun, to the harvest
that will feed the farmer, his brood, this village
and the next. But I must also paint the storm
that shades the sky, lifts a chill that breathes
little whispers on my skin – a sign
it's time to say goodbye to easy days.

Image: Ayesha Dharker

IMTIAZ DHARKER

Imtiaz Dharker grew up a Muslim Calvinist in a Lahori household in Glasgow, was adopted by India and married into Wales. She is an accomplished artist and video film-maker, and has published six books with Bloodaxe, *Postcards from god* (including *Purdah*) (1997), *I Speak for the Devil* (2001), *The terrorist at my table* (2006), *Leaving Fingerprints* (2009), *Over the Moon* (2014) and *Luck Is the Hook* (2018). She was awarded The Queen's Gold Medal for Poetry for 2014 and has also received a Cholmondeley Award from the Society of Authors and is a Fellow of the Royal Society of Literature. *Over the Moon* was shortlisted for the Ted Hughes Award for New Work in Poetry 2014. Her poems are on the British GCSE and A Level English syllabus, and she reads with other poets at Poetry Live! events all over the country to more than 35,000 students a year. In 2015 she appeared on the iconic BBC Radio 4 programme *Desert Island Discs*. In 2020 she was appointed Chancellor of Newcastle University. She lives in London.

SHADOW READER
BLOODAXE | £12.99 | PBS PRICE £9.75

According to an Indian tradition, gifted seers can predict a person's future by reading the shape of their shadow as it is cast upon a wall. One such prophecy haunts *Shadow Reader*'s lyric speaker, who in the poem 'But the radiance' is told "the year of (their) death" but "not how or where" it will happen:

> There was no way I could die
> at thirty-five or forty-five. I crossed murderous roads,
> ran red lights in rickshaws…

These poems are concerned with other's fates, too. The violent "rush of petrol" in 'Next' could take place in Mumbai or Manchester. Dowries remain legal in both parent countries, where "bride burning" and other abuses persist. 'For the Girl Whose Hair Escaped' satirically reports on institutional cover-ups, two years after Mahsa Amini's arrest and suspicious death in Iran for wearing her hijab "incorrectly":

> and out of nowhere the jaw
> comes apart and the teeth
> are lying on the floor

Weaving between her distinctive illustrations and powerful poems, Dharker expresses the most profound concern for humanity. Her sketched staircases might be prison bars, and the unyielding anaphora in 'Where you belong' queries both the addressee's freedom and our own:

> you can be in the group if you get enough likes,
> you can live with family if you toe the line,
> you can keep your children if we countersign

Served with a salty side dish of gallows humour, *Shadow Reader* is dissatisfied with speedy digital "sideways swipes" ('What it grows into') and tells humblebraggers to "Sod off" ('She Has an Off-day'). In a post-pandemic fling, William Blake ghosts one speaker who asks, "*Yo! Are you sick?*" whilst another streams footage of refugees carrying "bundles that cry like babies" ('Seen from a drone, Delhi'). Silences here drop like bombs or "a phone… on the face" ('Witness'). Compelled by the Donnian impulse to "make new shadows", the superbly woke poetry in this luminous collection is written wide "awake in the sonnet of a window".

SELECTOR'S COMMENT | JO CLEMENT

THE WELCOME

You were running on broken glass,
a child chased by nightmares
down battered streets, until at last
you came to this door. Here

are rooms made of hope, shelves full
of voices that call you in. They say
you can stop running now, pull
out a chair and sit. For you, they lay

a table with a feast that tastes of places
in your dreams, honey from the hive,
warm bread, words like spices.
This is where people come alive

to speak their stories in ink and blood
on wild nights, dappled afternoons,
telling of fallen tyrants, drought and flood
under desert stars and arctic moons.

They spin legends and conjure myths
in mother tongues and other tongues
that give your accent to their dance with death,
their love of life, the songs they sing.

You have been welcomed in
to books that smell like ancient trees,
standing here with broken spines,
opening like thoughts set free

and as the pages turn, your breath
quickens with something you always knew
in your blood like remembered faith.
When you open the book, it opens you.

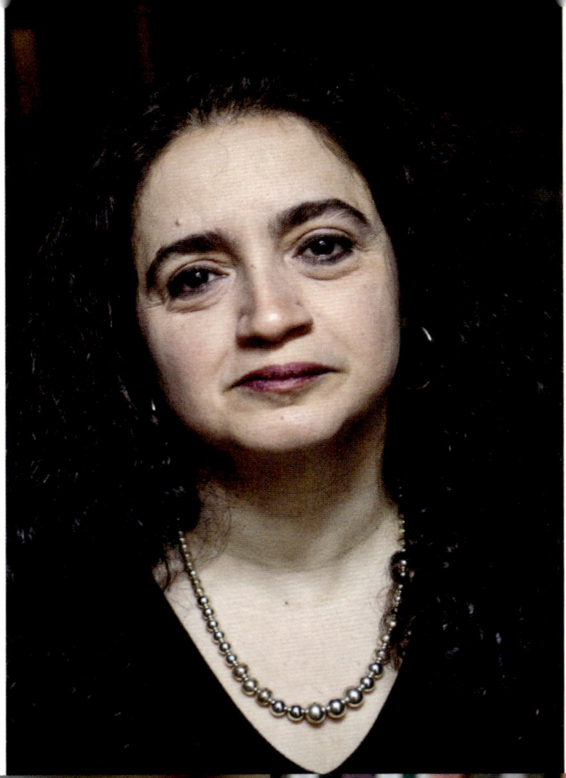
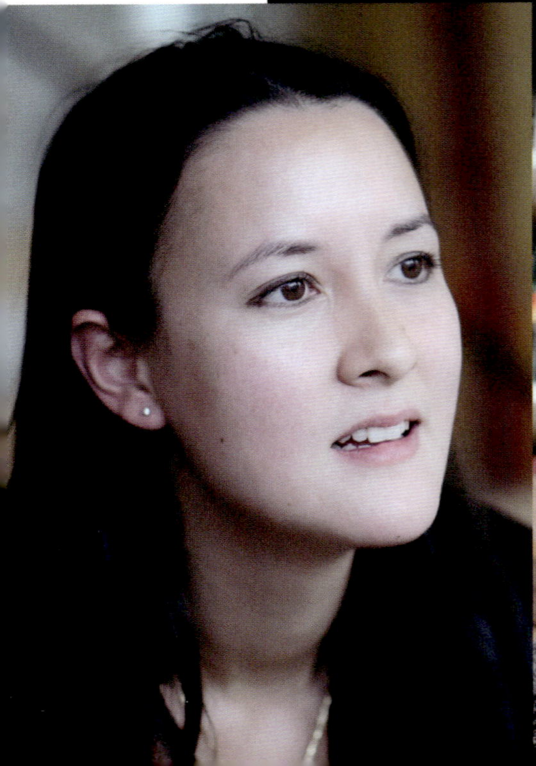
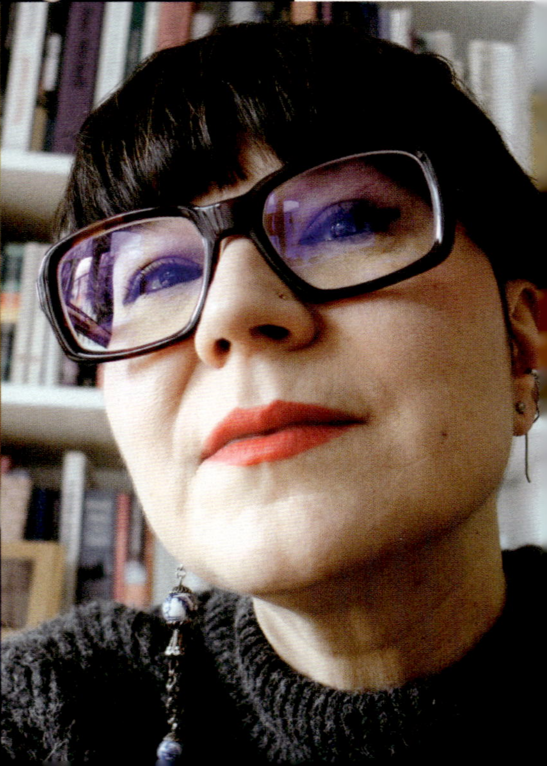

KARIN KARAKAŞLI

CANAN MARASLIGIL & SARAH HOWE

Karin Karakaşlı was born in Istanbul in 1972. She is the author of three poetry collections as well as several short story collections and novels, and co-writer of the research book *Armenians in Turkey: Community, Individual, Citizen*. With the Poetry Translation Centre she has previously published *History–Geography* (2017).

Canan Marasligil (she/they) is a writer, artist and literary translator in English, French, Turkish, Dutch and Spanish. Canan is also an advisor for het Cultuurfonds, a private Dutch fund supporting culture and nature, and a board member of the Dutch Writers Guild (Auteursbond). Canan shares new writing via the Attention Span newsletter and podcast (theattentionspan.com).

Sarah Howe is a British poet, academic and editor. Her debut *Loop of Jade* (Chatto & Windus, 2015) won the T.S. Eliot Prize and *The Sunday Times* / PFD Young Writer of the Year Award. Born in Hong Kong to an English father and Chinese mother, she moved to England as a child. She is now Poetry Editor at Chatto & Windus and a Lecturer in Poetry at King's College London.

REAL BY KARIN KARAKAŞLI
TRANS. CANAN MARASLIGIL & SARAH HOWE
POETRY TRANSLATION CENTRE | £9.00 | PBS PRICE £6.75

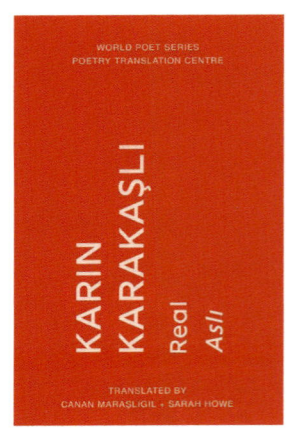

We are neither monuments to the horrors we have survived, nor carousels of our lives' vastest ebulliences: we are what observes, honestly, the constellated journey. So say the poems of *Real* by Karin Karakaşlı, translated from Turkish by Canan Maraşligil with Sarah Howe. *Real* is a gathering, not a sole incidence: it brings together poems written across Karakaşlı's fifteen-year career. Geographies of time move within the assembled work, accompanied by landscapes that bleed one into the other. Resolute from each poem to the next are first-person speakers who transfix us with an utter urgency.

Karakaşlı achieves this urgency by spry and unencumbered means. There is a directness to the poems rewarding those who long to hear the plain thing spoken directly, and with some beauty for its hardness. War and its unravelling shroud of displacement; the crisis of carrying rage within the body; unceasing vendettas borne out against women: *Real* houses these cares in a language that, without varnish, comes to the walled cities of the censorious and prises truth from its prisons. In 'Hair', the poet writes:

> They always strike at women through their hair
> where they're most naked
> Hair remembers
> the hands and faces once buried in it
> Hair will now call to mind
> the ones who gave up on themselves.

Unconquered hair surges in 'Gothic', the speaker telling us:

> There's a dark side
> to the ornaments on my face
> bitumen lining the eye like kohl
> tar wind at the roots of the hair.

Across *Real*, which will read as a journey you are walking – sometimes in purposeful strides, others on your knees, bereft – there are such inscriptions that embed the personal within the political, the everyday inside the life-altering. One shapes the other, Karakaşlı tells us. Indeed, it always has.

SHIVANEE RAMLOCHAN

I SELECTOR'S COMMENT

GOTHIC

My rebellion is a pointed and thin
prayer in the sky
I made patterns from memories alcoved
in my skin
Its stories are always thorny
My soul a sanctuary beaming with light
See that ray at the centre like a strip of tulle
Light that renders even the dust on the ground
sacred, like a magnet
My soul stirred memories
from particles of dust
They flew above me endlessly

My hope is the light of stained glass
transparent and shaded
At times blood red at times midnight blue
There's a dark side
to the ornaments on my face
bitumen lining the eye like kohl
tar wind at the roots of the hair
My elegance is an uncanny
gothic cathedral

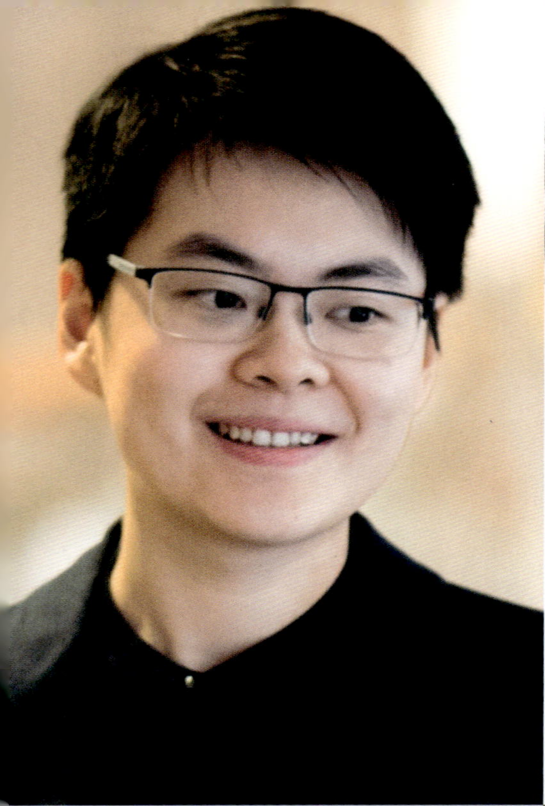
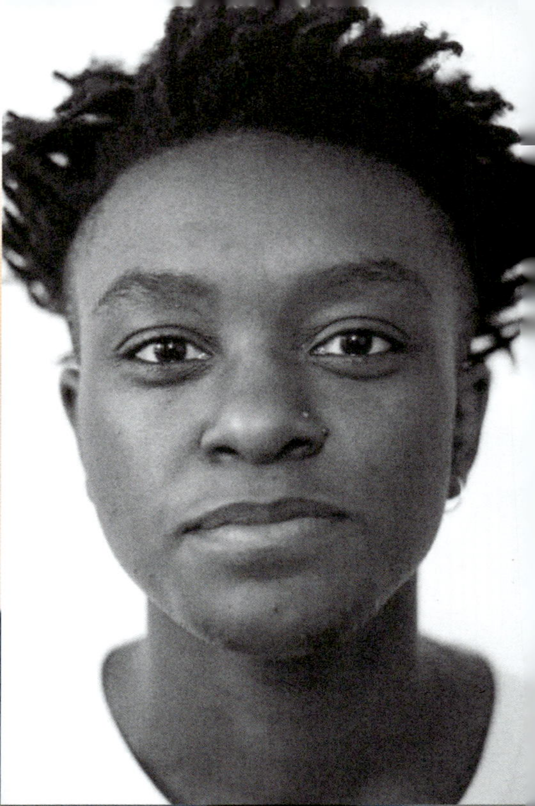
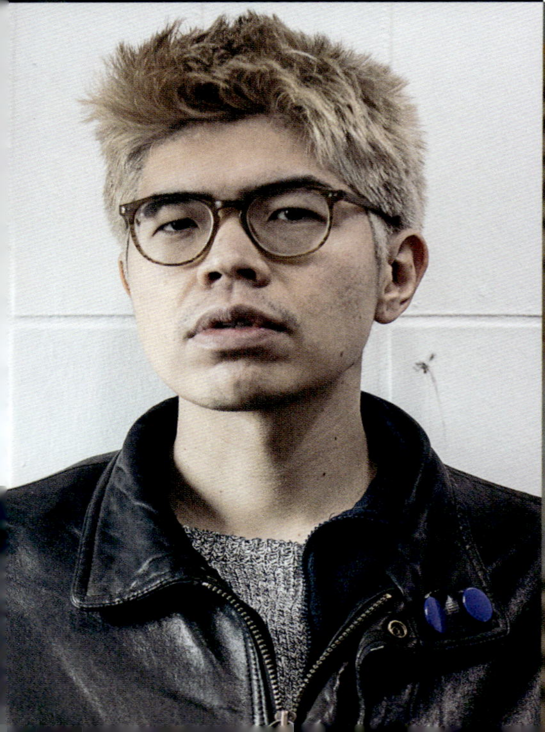
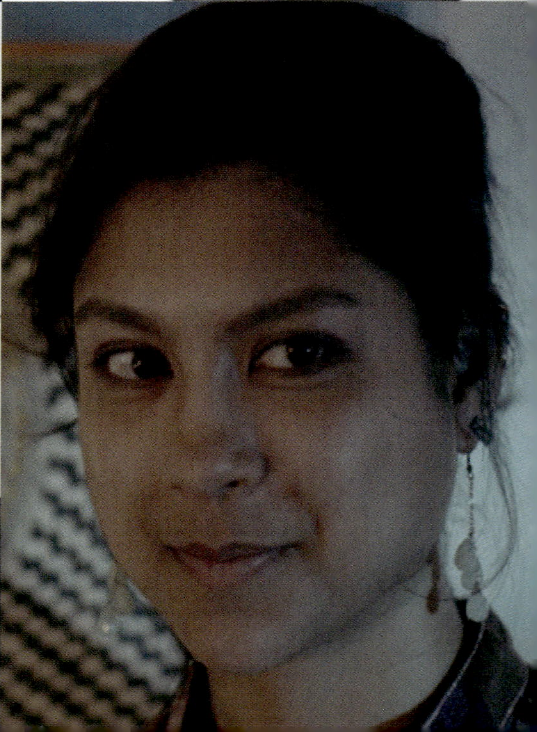

JAY BERNARD, MARY JEAN CHAN, WILL HARRIS & NISHA RAMAYYA

Jay Bernard (FRSL) is an interdisciplinary writer and artist from London whose work is rooted in social history. Their first collection *Surge* was based on the archives surrounding the New Cross Fire in 1981. Recent work includes *Blue Now*, a live rendition of Derek Jarman's film *Blue*, *Complicity* and a pamphlet about colonial memory in the urban environment. Jay is a DAAD literature fellow and a 2023/24 fellow at the Institute of Ideas and Imagination, Paris.

Mary Jean Chan is the author of *Flèche* (Faber, 2019), which won the Costa Book Award for Poetry and was shortlisted for multiple prizes, including the Seamus Heaney Centre First Collection Poetry Prize. Their second collection *Bright Fear* was a Poetry Book Society Recommendation and shortlisted for the 2023 Forward Prize for Best Collection. Chan is currently the Judith E. Wilson Poetry Fellow at the University of Cambridge and served as a judge for the Booker Prize.

Will Harris is the author of *RENDANG* (2020) and *Brother Poem* (2023), both published by Granta and *Mixed-Race Superman* (Peninsula). He was shortlisted for the T.S. Eliot Prize and won the Forward Prize for Best First Collection. He co-translated Habib Tengour's *Consolatio* (Poetry Translation Centre) with Delaina Haslam. He works in the care sector in Tower Hamlets, and helps facilitate the Southbank New Poets Collective with Vanessa Kisuule.

Nisha Ramayya grew up in Glasgow and now lives in London. Her poetry collection *States of the Body Produced by Love* (2019) is published by Ignota Books. Her second collection will be published by Granta in 2024. Tentatively called *Now Let's Take a Listening Walk*, it hazards a musical journey through history, myth, and sci-fi.

SIBLINGS
MONITOR BOOKS | £12.00 |

"I grew up with dual realities, with the knowledge of another reality occurring elsewhere," writes Will Harris in the opening pages of *Siblings*. The pamphlet begins with a transcript of a conversation between Will Harris, Jay Bernard, Mary Jean Chan and Nisha Ramayya. Drawing initially on Will Harris' collection *Brother Poem*, published in 2023, *Siblings* is a poetic conversation on notions of siblinghood in poetry, an idea which expands to touch on dual realities, diasporic memory, grief and queerness.

Composed of transcripts, childhood photographs and poems, *Siblings* possesses an intimate and immediate energy. *Siblings* captures what I love most about the pamphlet form and its radical possibilities: a sense of hybridity, play and physical movement across the pages. The poems feature brothers both real and imagined, and attempts to see them or be seen by them. As in Jay Bernard's 'After the cremation, I caught my brother smiling in the carpark':

> I saw unfolded levers pulling up his cheeks
> and pedals pressing tears out of his eyes.
> Then he put a hand up, so to hide,
> as everyone came filing to their cars.
>
> It's the mouth we cover first in laughter and in grief.

In Nisha Ramayya's vivid prose poem 'flower cup, seed vessel, wreath of words' the speaker imagines an attempt to reach their brother but instead refocuses on "the green hearts of the leaves" and their bodies of desire, where new, alternative forms of kinship emerge.

As poets we often discuss the lineage of our poems, but less so our poems' horizontal relationships: the threads and webs that connect them to other poets writing around us and with us, in similar physical, digital or emotional spaces. Mary Jean Chan recalls how their own thinking has been shaped by Harris' *Brother Poem*, and the conversation reveals further deep-rooted connections between all four poets. This pamphlet creates an intimate space for these "sibling poems" to dwell alongside each other, to speak to each other.

ARJI MANUELPILLAI & NINA MINGYA POWLES

AFTER THE CREMATION, I CAUGHT MY BROTHER SMILING IN THE CAR PARK

When I consider the evolution of the human,
I think of his mouth, like the bruised hoover
of the annelid, smiling against the earth
until its tip is flat like a sundial.
He was so much face.
His sweet skull bent from ball to plate.
I saw unfolded levers pulling up his cheeks
and pedals pressing tears out of his eyes.
Then he put a hand up, so to hide,
as everyone came filing to their cars.

It's the mouth we cover first in laughter and in grief.
Hand as gnomon, hand as shadow blade,
that casts the dark across the face,
and makes it two at once:
the upper and lower hours
that rotate a single stare,
such as what I glimpsed – a boy
laughing and crying on the grass.

SUMMER BOOK REVIEWS

JANETTE AYACHI: QUICKFIRE, SLOW BURNING
REVIEWED BY DAVE COATES

Ayachi's second collection has an obvious relish for the spectacular, either in its language – a broad, sumptuous, often painterly vocabulary – or its subject matter: earthquakes, grave robbings, bombs and wildfires. Not all such poems work – "Explosion", marking the accidental deaths of 218 people in Beirut lands awkwardly – but when the poem's curiosity, metaphor and momentum mesh, as in the rhapsodic 'isolated, together', it's a joy to be swept along. A fine book with a big heart and imagination.

APRIL | PAVILION | £10.99 | PBS PRICE £8.25

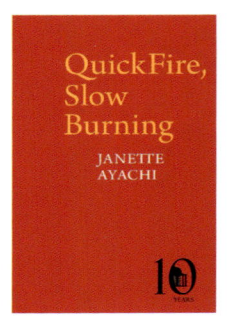

VERA CHOK: ANGRY YELLOW WOMAN
REVIEWED BY ANNIE FAN

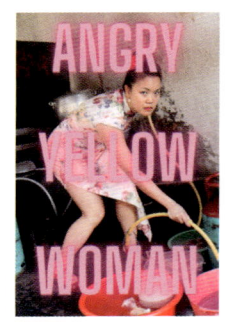

Vera Chok's poems are political first. Dialogues between Ted Hughes and Sylvia Plath, between 'Poetess 1' and 'Poetess 2' shift around with such great energy on the page that you can almost feel the poems speak. The typeset is consistently playful, the form defies any categorisation and straddles being part play script, part found poem. But Chok's best poems are the prose poems scattered throughout, with a tightness of theme and careful rhythm – where politics becomes art.

APRIL | BURNING EYE BOOKS | £9.99 | PBS PRICE £7.50

SAMANTHA FAIN: ARE YOU THERE
REVIEWED BY SHASH TREVETT

This is a collection rooted in the technological, phone driven, AutoCorrect world of the 21st century, which nonetheless speaks of the timeless pain of lost love and separation. Packed with beautiful imagery, ("rosy love sprawls to hibiscus"; "I look / at the moon & only see its cracks & craters") these poems negotiate the personal while interrogating the efficacy of poetry itself. Playful and despairing poems revolve around the figure of the absent "You" as the poet grieves for a "future we can't achieve".

APRIL | BAD BETTY PRESS | £10.99 | PBS PRICE £8.25

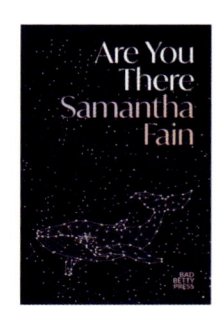

LEDBURY CRITICS

MELISSA LEE-HOUGHTON: EXPOSURE / IDEAL PALACE
REVIEWED DAVE COATES

Two books in one: the first in free verse with a grounded narrative voice, the second more formally regular but wildly surreal. This is a phenomenally ambitious project and it's credit to the poet that there are so few missteps, given its consistently electrifying emotional pitch. Reading it feels like passing through a loud, unpredictable, hyperstimulating inferno, led by a reassuringly witty Virgil. Lee-Houghton has achieved something unique, and worth experiencing.

MAY | PARIAH PRESS | £15.99 | PBS PRICE £12.00

AMELIA LOULLI: SLIP
REVIEWED BY DAVE COATES

Loulli's first collection examines the visceral realities of birth, motherhood and the medicalisation of women's bodies. The poems are bare, bold and declarative, drawing on the idioms of fairy tale, scripture and the medical textbook to great effect. A sequence on Loulli's own mother hits the mark beautifully. *Slip* is sometimes too indebted to Loulli's mentor, Fiona Benson, for its imagery and moods, but where it strikes out alone, it offers confidence, razor-sharp humour and a fine lyrical instinct.

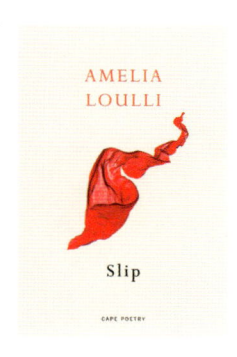

MAY | CAPE | £13.00 | PBS PRICE £9.75

POEMS AS FRIENDS: ANTHOLOGY
REVIEWED BY ROY McFARLANE

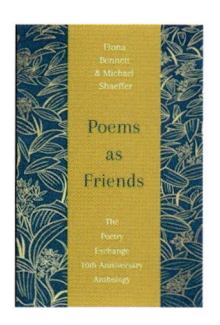

Poems As Friends, edited by Fiona Bennett and Michael Schaeffer, is more than a collection of poems, here poems become friends and individuals share that intimate journey. Sixty poems accompanied by sixty readers' stories of friendship; the good listener, the soul friend, the non-judgemental friend and more. From the layperson to the lover of poems, from poets to artists and actors, all partnered next to their poems of choice. You'll admire the stories, be challenged, be moved, be lifted, be loved and understand the beauty of poems as friends.

MAY | QUERCUS | £14.99 (HB) | PBS PRICE £11.25

| BOOK REVIEWS

ROWAN RICARDO PHILLIPS: SILVER
REVIEWED BY DAVE COATES

Statesman Phillips' fourth book is a frustrating read. An obviously gifted lyricist, the poems here rarely reach beyond pleasing soundscapes, neat syntactic twists and reversals. If you love Wallace Stevens you'll like *Silver*. But the book's constant allusion to Stevens (as he did in his excellent previous collection, *Living Weapon*) and his contemporaries, only foregrounds *Silver's* insubstantial feel, less composition than strumming, as in 'La Pulga', a poem about the footballer Leo Messi which doesn't quite earn its duration.

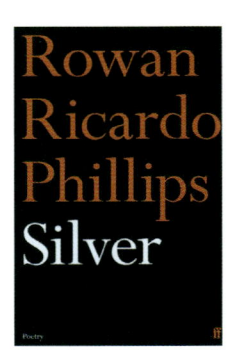

APRIL | FABER & FABER | £12.99 | PBS PRICE £9.75

KATRINA PORTEOUS: RHIZODONT
REVIEWED BY DAVE COATES

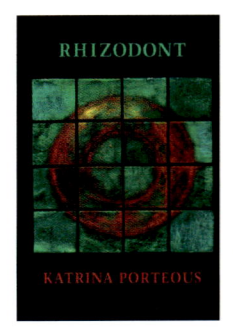

Rhizodont does for the mining and fishing communities of post-Thatcher Northumberland what Heaney did for mid-century Mid-Ulster, archiving the vast richness of its language, culture and work-lives. Porteous' painterly eye for detail gives depth and resonance to the histories and dramas of her human and non-human subjects alike. The ambitious second half, tackling speculative technologies and climate disaster, feels less weighty without the anchors of the first, but this remains a fascinating project, full of purpose and unexpected joy.

JUNE | BLOODAXE BOOKS | £12.99 | PBS PRICE £9.75

OKSANA MAKSYMCHUK: STILL CITY: DIARY OF AN INVASION
REVIEWED BY SHASH TREVETT

Charting the war in Ukraine (from waiting for the conflict to arrive to witnessing its horrors on the body, the mind, the city) these poems are both a tender and brutal examination of loss, confusion and dislocation. Important questions are asked of art, poetry and witness in beautifully crafted poems which "weave a language / out of things we felt / mattered". At a time where nowhere seems safe (a house, a memory, or even a poem), reading this collection seems vitally important.

MAY | CARCANET | £12.99 | PBS PRICE £9.75

ED. CHERRY POTTS & JEREMY DIXON: JOY//US
REVIEWED BY ANNIE FAN

It is easy to read these poems, easy to feel the lives behind them in the heady moments of bliss that this anthology captures. The editors "don't aim to answer" what queer joy is and yet there is a consistent celebration of hope and of comfort (in a body, in another body, in "cold pizza" or supermarket shopping), of having "no wish / to be anywhere else and no idea what comes next". What greater queer joy is there than to have the comfort, the ease, denied for so long?

MAY | ARACHNE PRESS | £9.99 | PBS PRICE £7.50

KASHIF SHARMA-PATEL: FURNISH, ENTRAP
REVIEWED BY DAVE COATES

This heady, rangy, challenging, playful debut is in dialogue with a burgeoning contemporary experimental tradition from Sean Bonney and Bhanu Kapil to Nat Raha and Nisha Ramayya. While a little opaque at times, its provocations – on the borderliness of British/Western culture, the transformative possibilities of Hindu and Buddhist philosophy and myth, how language shapes our reality – are handled with verve and warmth. They explain that, "we need a mythopoetics of the present": *furnish, entrap* contributes generously to that project.

APRIL | BROKEN SLEEP BOOKS | £11.99 | PBS PRICE £9.00

CHRISTINE ROSEETA WALKER: COCO ISLAND
REVIEWED BY SHASH TREVETT

This debut collection is filled with people living in and around Negril in Jamaica, who plough their own paths observed by a poet who sees all but refuses to spill secrets. "I'm not going to tell you" she says in poems which inhabit margins between the present and the past, the dead and the living, Christianity and the spell-casting of Obeah. Family and friends meander around each other in poems where words seem porous, allowing truth and meaning to migrate effortlessly into and out of lives.

APRIL | CARCANET | £11.99 | PBS PRICE £9.00

SUMMER PAMPHLETS

CHRISTOPHER ARKSEY: VARIETY TURNS

This elegiac pamphlet invokes the kitchen sink drama, not only in that herein is the stuff of the everyday, but also as Arksey has packed so much into this volume. Anecdotes and details pepper the pages, laying out grief through a variety of poetic forms. Holding as much fondness and admiration as sadness, this is a deeply human work.

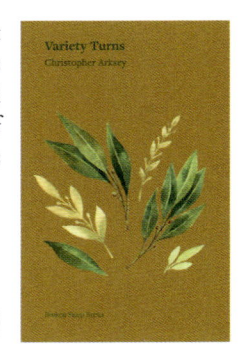

BROKEN SLEEP BOOKS | £8.99 |

ZOË BRIGLEY: LYCANTHROPE

Wolves walk in many guises through this chronicle of a long-distance love affair and the speaker's memories of violent men. Through this survey of wolves, Brigley explores sexuality and womanhood, considering these themes in threads of text messages, sent out often to no reply, which achieve a powerful intimacy even as they fly across time-zones. This is a striking work which asks who the real monsters are, and fixes them with a lupine eye.

SALÒ PRESS | £5.00 |

LAURIE BOLGER: MAKEOVER
REVIEWED BY REBECCA MORLEY

The 2023 Moth Prize winning poet Laurie Bolger balances the intimacy and warmth of childhood memory with a heart-wrenching exploration of womanhood. Bolger explores feminism through time and the complexity of the relationships in her life: her mother, her own body and men as a collective. *Makeover* perfectly presents the battles of life, as Bolger describes her body as "a jar of coins from places I don't remember visiting".

THE EMMA PRESS | £7.00 |

CORINNA BOARD: ARBOREAL

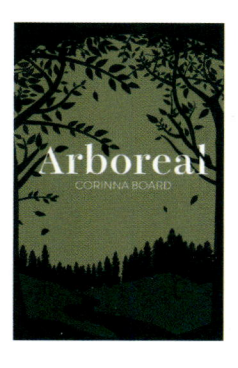

As the opening poem declares, "This is not a poem // it's a forest" *Arboreal* is not a pamphlet but a wooded way of being. Board leads us from seed to tree with sensory delight, from "a surprise of wild garlic" to the roots of Norse mythology in Askr and Embla, to the family trees and the "woods of the mind". This is nature reimagined – a tree holds a cosmos in its branches and silver birches are a "coven" – but all of it is rooted in a cautionary reminder of climate catastrophe: "today the last tree died".

BLACK CAT POETRY PRESS | £10.50 |

ELVIRE ROBERTS & RACHEL GOODMAN: KNEE TO KNEE

This bold collaborative pamphlet employs masterful linguistic play to effect an openness which makes space for the she-self to be, free as the children in photographs illustrating the title poem. While some poems eloquently consider serious subjects such as mental health and shame, the pamphlet as a whole is almost audaciously joyful; "there is / lightness and lifting / all the way up".

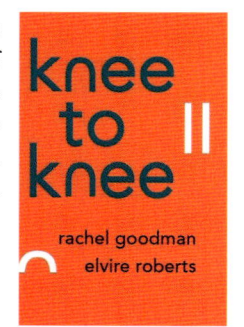

DIALECT PRESS | £10.00 |

SARAH WESTCOTT: POND

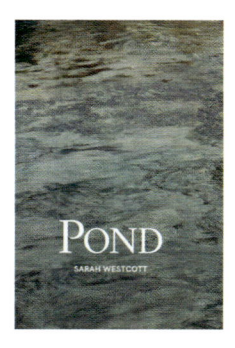

This beautifully produced pamphlet from the Braag by Sarah Westcott is full of "wet and complicated" wisdom. Water and words are called into being as the poet builds a pond and "this pond became a page". Westcott's poetry "pulses at the seams" of language, at the very edges of thought, bristling with thrilling newness, "submissive and haired". The pond itself is "full of mind" and we cannot help but pause, ponder and dip our toes into this immersive pool of thought.

THE BRAAG | £6.50 |

PAMPHLET REVIEWS

SUMMER BOOK LISTINGS

Kate Ashton	Matronymics	Shearsman Books	£10.95
Janette Ayachi	QuickFire, Slow Burning	Pavilion Poetry	£10.99
Yvonne Baker	Love Haunts in Shades of Blue	Cinnamon Press	£9.99
Harry Baker	Wonderful	Burning Eye Books	£9.99
Simon Barraclough	Divine Hours	Broken Sleep Books	£12.99
Caroline Bird	Ambush at Still Lake	Carcanet Press	£11.99
Sargon Boulus	Knife Sharpener	Banipal Publishing	£9.99
Eva Bourke	Tattoos	Dedalus Press	£11.00
John Burnside	Ruin, Blossom	Jonathan Cape	£13.00
Helen Calcutt	Feeling All the Kills	Pavilion Poetry	£10.99
Victoria Chang	With My Back to the World	Corsair	£12.99
Jos Charles	A Year and Other Poems	Broken Sleep Books	£11.99
Vera Chok	Angry Yellow Woman	Burning Eye Books	£9.99
Thomas A. Clark	That Which Appears	Carcanet Press	£17.99
Hannah Copley	Lapwing	Pavilion Poetry	£10.99
Ellen Cranitch	Crystal	Bloodaxe Books	£12.00
Amanda Dalton	Fantastic Voyage	Bloodaxe Books	£12.00
A. Dillon & J. Davidson	Downland	Two Rivers Press	£16.99
Grahame Davies	Darker Way	Seren	£10.99
Armen Davoudian	The Palace of Forty Pillars	Corsair	£10.99
Imtiaz Dharker	Shadow Reader	Bloodaxe Books	£12.99
Katie Donovan	May Swim	Bloodaxe Books	£12.00
Sasha Dugdale	The Strongbox	Carcanet Press	£12.99
Claire Dyer	Adjustments	Two Rivers Press	£11.99
Carrie Etter	Grief's Alphabet	Seren	£10.99
Samantha Fain	Are You There	Bad Betty Press	£10.99
Helen Farish	The Penny Dropping	Bloodaxe Books	£12.00
Kate Fox	Bigger on the Inside	Smokestack Books	£7.99
Harry Josephine Giles	Them!	Picador	£10.99
John Greening	From the East...	Renard Press	£10.00
Rob Hamburger	Nude against a Rock	Waterloo Press	£12.00
Matt Howard	Broadlands	Bloodaxe Books	£12.00
Rae Howells	This Common Uncommon	Parthian Books	£10.00
Alexander Hutchison	The Fusslin Thrang	Blue Diode Press	£10.00
Martha Kapos	Music, Awake Her	Two Rivers Press	£12.99
A. Kent & S. McPherson	All Empty Vessels	Broken Sleep Books	£12.99
Frank Kuppner	Not a Moment Too Soon	Carcanet Press	£11.99
Deborah Landau	Skeletons	Corsair	£10.99
Melissa Lee-Houghton	Exposure/Ideal Palace	Pariah Press	£15.99
Sylvia Legris	The Principle of Rapid Peering	Corsair	£10.99
Jenny Lewis	From Base Materials	Carcanet Press	£11.99
Amelia Loulli	Slip	Jonathan Cape	£13.00
Oksana Maksymchuk	Still City: A Diary of an Invasion	Carcanet Press	£12.99
Harry Man	Popular Song	Nine Arches Press	£11.99
Aoife Mannix	Reconstruction	flipped eye publishing	£8.95
J.L.M. Morton	Red Handed	Broken Sleep Books	£11.99
Stanley Moss	Goddamned Selected Poems	Carcanet Press	£16.99
Kristjan Norge	The Demon Tracts	Broken Sleep Books	£12.99
Mary O'Malley	The Shark Nursery	Carcanet Press	£11.99
Antony Owen	Post-Atomic Glossaries	Broken Sleep Books	£12.99
Alan Payne	Mahogany Eve	Smith|Doorstop	£10.99
Rowan Ricardo Phillips	Silver	Faber	£12.99
Katrina Porteous	Rhizodont	Bloodaxe Books	£12.99
Clare E. Potter	Healing the Pack	Verve Poetry Press	£10.99
J.H. Prynne	Poems 2016-2024	Bloodaxe Books	£25.00